Her Evolution Redefined

Practical Guide to Redefining Your Philosophy!

Mone' Wallace

Copyright © 2018 Nuance Publishing

All rights reserved. No part of this book may be reproduced or transmitted in any form or by any means, electronic or mechanical, including photocopying, recording or by any information storage and retrieval system, without written permission from the author, except for the inclusion of brief quotations in a review.

ISBN-13: 978-0692125120
ISBN-10: 0692125124
Printed in the United States of America

Table of Contents

Supporters		5
Introduction		7
Chapter 1	You Can't Do This Alone!	9
Chapter 2	Allow Me to Reintroduce Myself	11
Chapter 3	Mindset Makeover	15
Chapter 4	You Are the Sum of the Five	19
Chapter 5	Your Ideal Life	21
Chapter 6	Forgive Them for You	25
Chapter 7	Love you…NOW	29
Chapter 8	Your Philosophy	33
Chapter 9	Stop Waiting to Get Your Sh*t Together	37
Chapter 10	What If I Told You…	41
Chapter 11	Stop Giving Discounts!	44
Chapter 12	YOU are ENTIRELY up to YOU	48

A special thank you to my
Supporters

Drea McDonald

Portia Quaintance

Aubrey Pompey

Shameka Oakman

Terrence WIlson

Joy Brown

Drea McDonald

Brittany London

Kimberly "Isis" Thomas

Devonie Walker

Tavaris Beard

Larry Caldwell

Samantha Avera

Jessica Stephens

Jovita Smart

Brianna Pope

Ashley Cullars

Introduction

Hello, my name is Mone' Wallace and I am here to provide you with a few practical and proven steps to help you elevate your self-esteem and create a life designed by you.

In this book, I want to provide you with the very same steps that I took to become the woman that I am today.

My entire life changed when I got in tune with the God within. I began to learn so much about myself, my purpose, and how to live authentically and unapologetically. I learned how to overcome what was hindering my progression from living my very best life, as well as take the necessary steps to ensure that my past has no negative interferences with my future.

Today, I am a woman who is liberated in truth. I am no longer held captive of the thoughts and opinions of "the narrative." I am me and who I am is enough. I want you to feel this, know this, and believe this. Because you too are ENOUGH!

You are here because you are ready to embark upon this journey with me. I welcome you. All that I ask is that you open your mind, open your heart, and prepare to take action. Get ready to achieve and experience this radical life transformation!

"I am me. That is exceeding enough."

Chapter 1

You Can't Do This Alone!

When you are stepping into a realm of the unknown, it is scary! When you make the choice to live past expectations, it means that you are committing to step outside of your comfort zone and do something that you've never done before. You are spreading your wings and ready to leap into the unknown!

The vision that I have for my future now is so much bigger than what I could've ever imagined for myself just two years ago. My vision consists of things that I'd never imagined I would be doing (such as writing books). In 2015, I had a vision of me standing on stage pouring into a stadium filled with women! Confused, excited, doubtful and anxious, are the four emotions that had me fully overwhelmed with this vision. I had no idea where this derived from nor why I was seeing this, because I'd never seen myself being that important. My thoughts were more like "What in the world do I know that is valuable enough to share with anyone?" Truth is, I'd been living so comfortably within my expectations that it was hard for me to accept that my life could be anything more.

After seeing this vision and paying it no attention whatsoever, I continued on with life as usual. Just months later in November of 2015, I began to feel an unpleasant nudge in my gut. It felt really weird and very uncomfortable. At the time I had no idea what it was but my spirit led me to prayer. For seven days I took time to pray and truly focus on hearing God's voice. Eventually, I got clarity and direction. Two months later, I left Chicago, Illinois and moved back to my hometown of Augusta, Georgia. Unbeknownst as to why I was returning, I followed my gut and began my journey.

On this journey of the unknown, you are going to need direction from the one who called you to make a move, which is your Creator! It's impossible to live out the vision you were given without the direction from the one who created your path. Take time to pray, meditate, and tune in! These are all forms of communication with your Creator. In doing this, you will gain clarity, self-awareness, guidance, peace, joy, and so much more. You can truly have the life that you envision for yourself, if you first believe that it is possible to have.

I recommend having a regimen for everything! This is my way of disciplining myself, because I admit, I am horrible with remembering to do things. However, setting a regimen or formula that allows me to repeat the activity daily, brings ease to the task at hand as well as poses a great reminder to get it done.

My daily regimen for my spiritual relationship consists of three main things:

1. *Start and end the day with prayer.*

    I spend 10-15 minutes just talking and thanking God for everything. The water, the trees, my family, the lessons that we learn in life. I also journal these prayers in my gratitude journal.

2. *Meditate for 20 minutes.*

    Sit or lie comfortably. Close your eyes and breathe. Make no effort to control your breath, simply breathe. Be easy on yourself, your mind will wander. Let it, don't force anything. The purpose for your meditation is to hear from your Creator so you'll want to make this process as calm as possible. Meditation can also help us to understand our own mind. We can learn how to transform our mind from negative to positive, from disturbed to peaceful, from unhappy to happy.

3. *Journaling.*

    One thing that I do know for sure is that when our Creator has revealed something to us, She is not required to repeat it! So write it down! Every idea, vision, strategy, word, or quote that is downloaded into your spirit, write it down!

> "If you can't figure out your purpose, figure out your passion. For your passion will lead you right into your purpose."
>
> *T.D. Jakes*

Chapter 2

Allow Me to Reintroduce Myself

Who are you really? Is the question that I had begun to ask myself one year ago. Upon embarking on this journey of self-development, I knew that I wasn't living in the full capacity of who I was truly created to be and that alone set the tone for me to put in some work!

Self-awareness saved my life. When I started learning more about who I truly am and who I am becoming, it was scary. I had begun to learn simple things like what I really like to eat versus what I only ate because someone I dated ate it. Also things like, I really love being, feeling, and looking sexy. This has always been me but overtime I allowed my peers, family and boyfriends to shame this side of me. So I had to retrain my mind as a whole to really accept who I am and to be okay with being who I am in front of the world. This has been a challenge because I was always the "people pleaser." I had always lived to please my friends and the guys I dated. But now that's all changed!

Now I have a clear vision of the woman I am now and the woman I am becoming. Now I have done the self-work to heal from my past and take accountability over my life. Now I am taking full responsibility for my happiness and my life because I recognize my value. When you find out how valuable you really are, you stop giving people discounts.

So how do you go about finding your value? How do you begin to recognize how amazing you truly are? You spend time alone, a lot of it. Isolate yourself and heal from situations that have kept you feeling angry, bitter and unforgiving. Give your heart a chance to breathe. Take some pressure off of your spirit. This is a process, allow it to be that. Also, you remind yourself of how dope you are. Make a list and keep it very visible. Sticky notes are my life! I have my mantras all over my house! This self-love thing is real, hunni', and it's a journey. A muscle that needs exercise daily.

Get clarity! When I started setting boundaries in my life, it allowed me the time to gain clarity in what was necessary and needed, but missing in my life. I became clear about my actions and reactions. I've learned to listen, respond, and then react. I've learned that it's okay to allow yourself to feel. Many women, like myself, have experienced some sort of trauma in life that caused us to be more masculine in our emotions than feminine. We are born with both emotions so it's certainly not that difficult to transition between the two. However, being more masculine than feminine shadows the essence of the nurturer that we were created to be. When we delve into the masculine energy, it aids us in being less vulnerable and we shut out our emotions that allow us to love freely and openly.

I'm just speaking from my experience. Because of my past, I'd become accustomed to "shutting down my feelings." I had a few ex's to tell me that it was like turning a light switch on and off. And like the naive girl that I was, I thought it was my magic! I thought that being able to shut down my feelings so dramatically was a super power that I could use to control situations. But in retrospect, I was just a girl that was suffering from her past and had learned to protect her heart by any means necessary. After being raped at the age of fourteen and having no support whatsoever, I learned how to disassociate my feelings from people and their actions. Being raped changed my view of people. From the way that I treated and trusted people to the way that I carried myself when I was in a setting full of strangers. I thought that I'd mastered the true art of not giving a f**k, because I was able to shut down so effortlessly.

A part of self-love is being able to question and honestly answer yourself. This process helped me to recognize "my why" behind my actions. I had to face the situation as a grown woman and allow myself to feel the emotions all over again. I processed the situation, the emotions, the people involved, and then I forgave. I chose to forgive my rapist, his sisters who watched, and everyone who chose not to believe me…even my family. In doing so, I gained so much power and knowledge of who I truly am. I am NOT a woman who is afraid of emotions, trust, or love. I am a lover, a nurturer, a caregiver, and a hopeless romantic. I am a woman who is fully aware of her being! I am in love with love, I have unique gifts, I am feminine with a dab of gangsta, my talents are purposeful, and my purpose is the reason I breathe. I am an amazing being! I am one DOPE Queen! And so are you!

I am so thankful for my journey, because it has helped me to see myself for who I truly am rather than who I once thought I was. Back then, I was lost in the comfortability of my circumstances and my past. But now I have become a better version of myself and I am living life like it's golden! To me, love is a deep appreciation. When I talk about loving self, I mean having a deep appreciation for who you are; in which you accept all the different parts of you, your peculiarities, the embarrassments, the things you may not do so well, and all the wonderful qualities. Self-discovery is a beautiful journey and I invite you to join me on the journey. I promise to hold your hand and provide you with the encouragement and guidance needed along the way

Here, I've listed three steps that I took to start my journey of self-love. It is good to revisit this often as a friendly reminder.

1. *Accept the entire package with unconditional love.*

    You are perfectly imperfect. You are beautiful, even in your insecurities. Your freckles are right where they should be. You are a gem created from royalty, nothing about you is out of place. Love every part of you. You are not perfect, you will make mistakes. Learn to laugh at them. Mistakes are here to help us learn, embrace them. You are forgiven for everything that you have done and will do. (He gave His only begotten son). Now forgive yourself, often.

2. *Be accountable.*

    Self-love is a process. You must decide if this is the journey for you, because it means that you are committing to being authentic with yourself and others. It means that you take accountability for your actions and reactions. It means that you rid yourself of excuses, because they only hinder your progress.

3. *Know what you deserve.*

    You deserve all that your heart desires. You deserve to be loved unconditionally. You deserve to be swept off of your feet by the person that you have the hugest crush on. You deserve to go on walks alongside the beach while holding hands and having intellectual conversations. You deserve to be taken on spontaneous dates with the love of your life. You deserve all of the love that you wish to have, and it will come. But first, you must give it to yourself.

> *"Authenticity requires vulnerability, transparency, and integrity."*
>
> — *Janet Louise Stephenson*

Chapter 3

Mindset Makeover

When you see yourself differently, you begin to think differently. There's a shift that happens in your mind and it brings clarity to the true power that you possess. Your journey to becoming your true self will also include you questioning your beliefs. For me, I'd begun to question my beliefs about everything! I wanted to learn more about my past, about my religion, about my decisions and the reasoning behind them. I was determined to fully discover who I am and why.

Your life is an indication of the way that you believe, and my life was reflecting that I had a lacking mindset. I believed in so many things that were holding me back from believing outside of my circumstances. I didn't believe that I could ever write a book. I didn't believe that people would ever be interested in what I had to say. I didn't believe that I'd ever be impacting lives, but you'd be amazed at what can happen when you answer the calling on your life.

What changed my mindset about life was traveling. The first time I got out of my comfort zone was in 2012 when I moved to Atlanta. I moved with a friend and she was the only person that I knew. She then brought me around her friends who were all actors, teachers, lawyers, and entrepreneurs. This was the most intimidating time of my life. I felt like I was definitely in the wrong place. There I was just a young girl from the hood who didn't even have a high school diploma. I thought to myself, "What in the world do I have in common with any of these people?" I knew that if this was going to be my circle, I was going to need to level up in my thinking.

Over time, I ventured out to try new things. I ate Thai and Hawaiian food for the first time. I also ate my first expensive a** steak at Ruth's Chris, but it was one of the best steaks that I've ever had. I met people that I would have never been open to meeting, I made friends who were from different countries, I'd experienced things that I'd never thought I'd be interested in, and come to find out, I love these things. Things like mountain climbing and painting, also reading and studying my culture, learning about investments and chakras. My mind was exposed to so many new things that it allowed me to think and believe in another dimension. My mental capacity was exceeding far past my comfort zone and I just went with the flow, enduring all of the knowledge, good vibes, and positive energy in my atmosphere.

From there, I made the decision to get back into school as well as learn different skills. Eventually, I plan to learn new languages, but one thing at a time (lol). After Atlanta, I lived in Chicago. Now while this was only for a brief period of time, I enjoyed every moment learning the diversity and culture that existed there. The city was cold, in climate and in truth. Although the city is lit with beauty, it's covered in hate and it's saddening. When I lived there I hated to even turn on the news, because I was sure to feel drained after watching. But it was totally different when I went out into the city. Downtown had some of the best restaurants. My favorite was Gino's East! The best pizza you will ever eat.

Traveling also helped me to see that there was so much more to life than what I'd been settling for. All I knew was what I had been exposed to, but when I decided to travel and experience life differently, my mind shifted. I had a complete mindset makeover.

4 Benefits of Traveling

1. *Improves Social and Communication Skills*

   One of the main benefits of traveling, especially to areas where your native language is not widely used, is that you learn how to communicate with all manner of different people. It could be communicating to find the way to your next destination or asking for the nearest restaurant.

2. *Ensures Peace of Mind*

   We all have stress and tension in our lives. Traveling forces us to temporarily disconnect from our normal routine and it helps us appreciate the people and things you have around. As per a famous saying, "We never know what we have until we lose it."

3. *Broadens Your Horizons*

   Traveling helps you connect with different people from different cultures, and this is fatal to prejudice, bigotry, and narrow-mindedness. Meeting people from different cultures and societies will help you see issues and daily life from many different angles.

4. *Boosts Up Your Confidence*

   Being in a place where you do not know anyone will assist you to gain confidence and presence of mind. You will develop the ability to cope with obstacles, which will make you a confident person and help you grow as a person.

Name three places you want to visit. Include why you want to visit and when you plan to visit.
(Don't think about your finances, just write.)

"I'm starting to attract exact type of people I want around me; creative minds with amazing commitment to their dreams."

Unknown

Chapter 4

You Are the Sum of the Five

Chasing your dreams requires a lot! You are consistently going to be facing life! Obstacles get in the way, people become distractions, the 9-5 becomes a hassle, and we end up feeling drained. These are the days when I count on my riders. My girls that are there to lift me up past my sorrows and speak life into me. These are women that encourage me to keep going! They remind me of who I am and the power that I possess. The resilience and the confidence that they all embody are beautiful and necessary.

However, this was not always the case. In my past, I've had friends that didn't wish me well and want the best for me. They actually prayed for my downfall and spoke negatively about things that I wanted to do. This was discouraging and hurtful; but at the same time, it was very eye opening. Those experiences were necessary and from them I learned so much. When others don't understand your vision, do not get angry with them. After all, the vision was not given to them. Therefore, it is ok for them to misunderstand and some will even doubt your ability just because they doubt their own. Do not allow this to intimidate or stop you, keep going!

Also, being a sum of your five means that you cannot be the smartest in your circle. As you evolve, you will continue to level up in all aspects of your life. Your conversations will change, your interests will change, and your taste in life will change. You will begin to hunger for more knowledge of yourself, your likes and interests, as well as your crafts. It is imperative that you are not the smartest person in your circle. As you think, so will they! You need to center yourself in a circle where you can learn above the capacity that you are used to learning. This journey will reveal so much about not only who you are, but also who you are becoming. Prepare now for where you are going. Be intentional about the connections that you make, as these will influence your thoughts and your decision making. Becoming the best version of you so that you may live your best life includes your atmosphere, your energy, and your visuals. Make sure that you are consuming the necessities that feed your growth.

As you continue to evolve into this higher version of yourself you will realize that everyone who started with you may not end with you. This doesn't mean that you will lose them as a friend, however, you may begin to notice that the things that once interest you no longer do. And the places that you used to hangout are no longer fun. This could cause a problem if your friend(s) have remained stagnant. As they may find your changes offensive and this could cause a drift in the friendship. Yes it may hurt at first but always remember, some people are in our life for a reason and some for a season. Enjoy the moments and the lessons, but don't allow the outcome to make you mad or bitter. Everyone isn't ready to grow and go with you!

Think about where you want to be five years from now. What type of friends do you need to have now that will help you get to where you are going? *(Consider character)*

"Even if it's not your ideal life, you can always choose it. No matter what your life is, choosing it changes everything."

Andre Agassi

Chapter 5

Your Ideal Life

Have you ever taken a moment to think about your ideal life? When you close your eyes and envision yourself being in a happy place, what does this look like? Does this include material things such as cars, homes, and clothes? Possibly you spending days away on vacation with bae or a family trip? What is the life that you envisioned for yourself as a young girl? If you're anything like me, then as a young girl you had a wild imagination and you knew that your dreams were limitless! Then overtime life happens and we begin to lose sight of the vision and we no longer use our imagination. From day to day we just begin living our reality, the here and now. For a moment think about this, if you could begin living your ideal life today, what would it look like?

As a young timid girl, the vision of my future self was to be the type of woman who had so much power and poise. One who would be authentic, relentless, courageous and would stand up for what she believed in. She wouldn't bite her tongue when crossed and would read you with grace in the blink of an eye. She would be high maintenance, but still a lil' hood or as I like to say "boughetto." This was a clear vision and today I can proudly say that I am becoming more and more of that woman every day.

I envisioned my future self then and I still do now. As I've learned, it's so important to know where you are going so that finding your way won't be so difficult. In fact, I even keep an "ideal life" journal. This is where I keep my life vision notes. I truly believe in having a vision and being intentional about keeping it in front of me. In this journal I express the vision of my ideal life. Things like "I look forward to waking up in my dream home and hearing the sound of the beach as I open my eyes. The beautiful sunrise greets me through the view of my patio, awakening me and my love."

Whatever the vision is that you have for your life, I encourage you to put it down on paper. Studies show that you become 42% more likely to achieve your goals and dreams, simply by writing them down. Also know that it takes more than just putting it down on paper, you also have to believe that you are worthy of having these things. For example; It is impossible to envision having the love of your life sweep you off of your feet when you are operating from a broken place and unable to give or receive love. When your heart is broken, you are going to attract broken hearted people.

When envisioning your ideal life don't be afraid to write what you truly want. Don't think about what other people would think or say. Don't allow your doubts and fears to keep you from thinking big. Just imagine, feel, and write. Connect your emotion with the vision. How does it feel? Smell? What does it look like? Who is included? Where are you? What are you doing? What is life like in your imagination? Everything that can come to mind I assure you it's yours. If only you can believe that it is yours and you are willing to do whatever it takes to make it happen. No matter what, never stop dreaming and never give up on making your dream your reality.

Write the vision, make it plain. What does your ideal life look like?

_____

_____

Who do you need to become to acquire this life?

What can you do today that will get you one step closer to this life?

"It doesn't matter who I used to be. All that matters is who I've decided to become."

Mone' Wallace

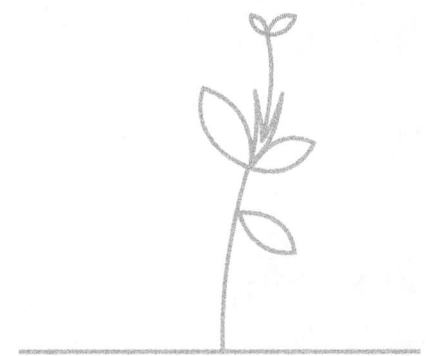

Chapter 6

Forgive Them for You

I used to be so angry and upset asking God, "Why me? Why did my life have to be so hard?" I experienced a rather rough childhood. I was always getting into trouble, being suspended from school, getting into fights, and having disagreements with my family. I was a very misunderstood and tempered child. I was a middle child and the baby girl, but I caused the most hell.

I got into trouble consistently and was finally sentenced to 60 days in a juvenile justice system at the age of 16. There I met a lot of other troubled teen girls. This experience is one that I will never forget. From the beds to the bathrooms and the food, yuck! This was definitely not a place for me. I absolutely hated it and I could not wait to go! I made a calendar and began counting the days, but it seemed to make the time pass even slower. So, I eventually just gave up and decided to wait it out, as if I had any other choice.

In retrospect, I can truly say that I appreciate this experience, because it taught me so very much about life! I learned how to be calm tempered and patient. It taught me how to get along with other girls, because that's something I've always struggled with. It taught me how to be more of a positive leader than a negative one. I became very close with an officer there and I believe to this day that she was my guardian angel. The way that she cared for me when I was in that place was remarkable! She disciplined me and checked me when I was wrong, but loved on me when I needed love. She was my light in that time of darkness and I will never forget her.

I also questioned things like my rape and molestation and why after those experiences I became more interested in sex. I became more open and aware to my surroundings and I learned how to seduce and manipulate for anything that I wanted. I wondered why I was able to live the life that afforded me a lot of nice things, but diminished my self-worth. And then I got my answer. My life was formed by the choices that I made. God gave us all free will and how we choose to live has consequences. For me, God had grace and kept me alive in the midst of the deadliest and most dangerous situations so that I could be the voice of those who need to see hope! To hear that it is possible to live life and make mistakes, because God is going to use your past for your purpose! Because of the life that I lived I became very unhappy and depressed. I lost myself in a bad relationship and always looked for validation from everyone except me. That was, until the day I finally decided to stop feeling sorry for myself, forgave myself, and began to rebuild.

In my self-love process, when I began to forgive my past hurts and myself, I began to gain my power back. The power that allowed me to be vocal about my needs, wants, and truths. I also began to look at my life in another light. I went from being angry and feeling like the helpless victim, to claiming victory over my life and accepting that my testimony wasn't for me. It was to be shared to help the lives of others. And honestly, when I realized that, it filled my heart with joy. I thought to myself "Wow, God loves me so much that He walked with me through it all and brought me out on the winning side just to have a story that I can help save and transform lives with!" My GOD!

We all have a story that needs to be heard. Each of us have had our flavor of life and how we deal or don't deal will determine how we live the rest of our lives. For example, had I not forgiven my past heartbreak, I'd still be bitter and angry. I'd be allowing him to have control of my energy, because that's what my focus would be. But because I've forgiven him and myself, I am now very aware of who I am, what I have to offer and who isn't qualified to sit and dine at the table with me. So I encourage you today, forgive whoever for whatever, and watch how your joy begins to blossom.

Here is where I would like for you to take a moment to reflect. Place this book face down, take a deep breath, close your eyes, and sit in complete silence. Think about your past and everyone involved. Who do you feel has hurt or wronged you? Who has stolen your joy, peace, or hope? Can you see them? Good, now look them in the eye and say, "I FORGIVE YOU AND I FORGIVE ME. I RELEASE YOU AND I RELEASE ME. I THANK YOU FOR THE EXPERIENCE AND I AM NOW RECLAIMING MY POWER."

BREATHE...

Now, list the names of the people that you've forgiven. Once you're done, you can do one of two things. 1) Burn the list or 2) write those names on a balloon and release it into the sky. Truly rid yourself of the thoughts, the hate, the bitterness, the regret and the hurt. You deserve to be happy and it starts here, with you, right now.

"I approve of myself. In this moment, I embrace me and I appreciate me. I love myself deeply and fully!"

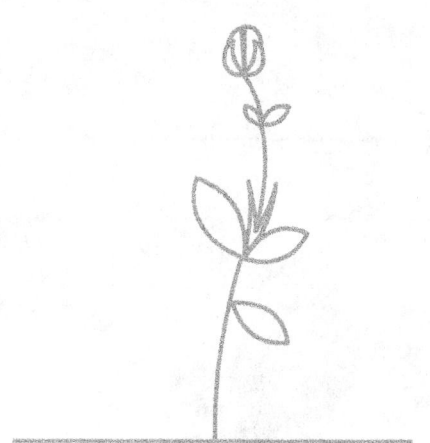

Chapter 7

Love you...NOW

What's funny to me is that I've told myself for years that I loved myself. I thought it was something as simple as looking in the mirror and saying, "Hey beautiful, I love me some you!" I also thought that it meant to keep your hair and nails done and always step out looking presentable. Now, granted these are a few ways to make yourself feel good. But there's a huge difference between just feeling good and loving yourself unconditionally.

For a very long time, I thought that I was happy with myself. I never once stopped to ask what true happiness felt like, or how I knew that I was happy. I just assumed that I was happy. It's funny how we learn from society that looking a certain way means that you love yourself. People will overspend and go completely broke just to make sure that they are flawless from top to bottom only to impress people who don't care anyway.

Yep, I was one of those people! Always spending money on the material pleasures but never understanding what "investing in myself" really meant.
I noticed that the girls and women that I idolized seemed to have it all so maybe if I portrayed that look, I'd have it all too. Or at least look like I did.

I then matured and assumed that loving yourself meant that you spoke affirmations and positivity all day. And that you value your time, space, and energy at all costs. Well, while all of this is true, that's not the end all be all!

I know you've all heard it before, "Self-love is being positive all the time. Self-love is always being happy and bubbly." Well allow me to disrupt that narrative. Self-love is simply accepting that you are imperfect as hell. Self-love is when you accept the fact that you're going to make mistakes, you're going to get upset and say things, you're going to have times where you remember the past; and for a brief moment you allow yourself to slip into familiar feelings. It's okay. Be fully aware of what you're feeling in that moment and know that it is okay, that it's not going to last, and that you should take solace to that moment. Our feelings are there to tell us something, signal something, and let us know that we need to pay attention. Many of the emotions that I stopped to pay attention to led me back to places in my past where I needed to forgive in order to move forward. Remember, even in our darkest moments come the brightest revelations. Something that may seem to be horrible right now, can be utterly refreshing and unexpectedly the very thing that we needed to propel us into our greatness. Pay attention to your feelings.

We all tend to get caught up and thinking that life is supposed to be perfect. That is not true. If you're thinking like that, STOP it! That's torture. Expecting yourself to serve at one hundred percent greatness at all times is bullsh*t. Don't stress yourself any more than you have to. Here's why: self-love is accepting YOU, flaws and all. It means being able to get into an argument and hang up on someone and allow yourself to be in your feelings.

And when you come out of that moment, I want you to question yourself. Question the situation. Ask yourself, why did this person say the things that they said? Why did you say the things that you said? What happened to spark this argument? And what could I learn from this? There's so much knowledge to be learned in making mistakes. There's so much wisdom in not always doing the right thing, but just doing something.

The most amazing thing about my journey of self-love was being able to know that it is possible to just be human. It is possible to make mistakes, it is possible to fall down, and it is possible to press the reset button as many times as I need to. Self-love is true liberation and it is good for the soul.

Here are three ways that you can begin to practice LOVING YOU NOW.

1. *Do something you're good at.*

    If this isn't the ultimate self-esteem booster, I don't know what is! Self-esteem and self-love often go hand in hand, and participating in a hobby you're good at will not only boost your endorphins, but will bring out the best version of you. If you love to cook, then cook! If you love to run, then grab those sneakers, head outside and run for your life.

2. *Find your happy place.*

    Think of a place that makes it simple to just be. That means being able to sit quietly and embrace the here and now. Not thinking about what's due at work or what bills need to be paid. You owe this happy place to yourself. Self-love is all about connecting with yourself, and one of the easiest places to do that is your happy place.

3. *Build your letting go muscle.*

    We're constantly holding on to things in our past, and it can tend to weigh heavy on our souls and even lower our self-esteem. The more blocks we clear, the more we can really live big in the area of self-love. Although we may do this as a way to protect ourselves from hurting, it's really only holding us back from moving forward to reaching optimal self-acceptance and loving who we are.

Change is never easy. Because as we evolve and our minds expand, we begin to see life in a new light. This light is one that you may or may not have seen spiritually, but when it manifests in your life, the feeling is impeccable. I want you to experience this evolutionary shift. I want you to WIN. I want to witness you experience your wildest dreams become a reality! So I assure you, nothing GREAT can come to you while you are living in your comfort zone. It is time for the world to see you shine! You were born with such brilliance and I refuse to let you settle for anything less than what makes your soul say YES.

What radical changes will you commit to in order to stay consistent on your journey?

*Be in love with your life...
every minute of it!"*

Jack Kerouac

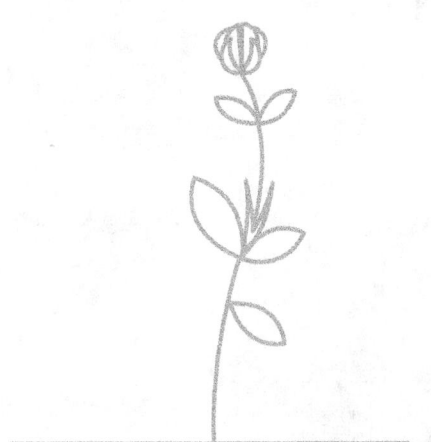

Chapter 8

Your Philosophy

What is the guiding principle for your behavior? What are your beliefs and why? What were you "taught" as an adolescent? Does it feel like truth or tradition? These are a few of the questions that I asked myself when I started this journey. I knew that if my goal was to find out who I am at my core, I'd have to explore why I thought the way that I did. When I started to ask these types of questions I also had to be open to changing my belief system, and I have.

When I hear the word philosophy, it makes me think of the freedom to be! I honor the truth of who I am and I exalt in the freedom from the weight of the world and their opinions about my life. I am the narrator of my story, I am in control of directing my movie, and the world is simply my audience. If they like the showing, they'll stay for more. I If they don't, they'll leave the theater. But all in all, it is mine to create!

I am grateful for each moment that I am able to breathe. I am grateful for being in love with myself, flaws and all. I am most impressed with my imperfections, because they set me apart and I love being different. I am thankful for the freedom to live my wildest dreams and the confidence to know that I can have it all! I am elated to experience freedom at such a high level that it attracts alike individuals. To be fulfilling to the needs of your core truth and honoring the love criteria for your life is my definition of self-love.

As you begin this journey of redefining yourself, understand that each day is a process. Each day will not be perfect but remember to always look for the good. Perception is everything. And our mind arrives at a place faster than our physical body. So if you can see the good in any situation and continue to feed your mind and soul with the richest of words, you are setting the best intention for your outcome.

You deserve to have the life that you've envisioned so many times. You were created to live a fulfilled and abundant life. Everything that you've always wanted is available to you. The career, the car, the man, the kids. Whatever you can imagine you absolutely can have! But can you handle the life that you are praying for? This is the real question.

When I began my journey to discovering who I really was, I had to go deep. I had face things that I didn't want to relive, as well as forgive along the way. I had to forgive myself for the things that I said to myself and accepted. I had to stop being the victim and take accountability for my actions. In doing this, I've learned how resilient and loving I truly am, also how feminine and soft I am. I learned that I am enough no matter what. My beauty nor my clothes define me, nor does my hair or bank account. What defines me is what I think about me! My beautiful qualities and the value that I add to the lives of those around me. This is truly what it's about for me. I encourage you to do the same, take full advantage of life every day and make it nothing short of amazing. True enough, everyday won't be easy. But keep in mind you have control. You can't control a situation, but you can control your reaction to it.

Take solace to your inner beauty for a second. You are created from greatness, therefore you are greatness. Never forget this and walk in this proudly. You are a Queen. A daughter of the most high and your truest self awaits you

QUESTION

What radical changes are you willing to make to become the highest version of yourself?.

Are you ready to get out of your comfort zone?

What are three things that need to happen this week to get you one step closer to your biggest goal?

What does life on your terms look like?

*"I have all that I need to succeed in this life.
Right now is the perfect moment to express
my gratitude for all that I have.
All that I possess is enough."*

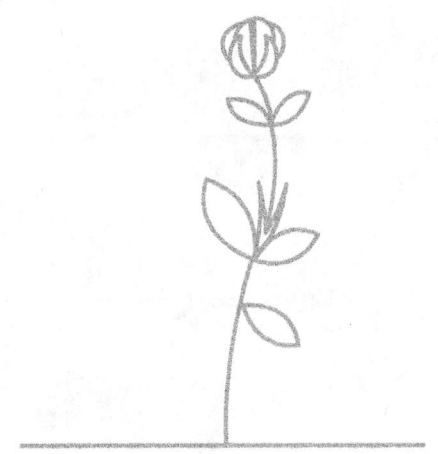

Chapter 9 | Stop Waiting to Get Your Sh*t Together

It took me a very long time to finally stop making excuses and just do something. We miss out on many great opportunities, simply because we are "waiting" until we get our sh*t together, in order to get our sh*t together.

How many of us are guilty of this? "I'll start my business when I save some money." "I'll be happy once I drop 30 pounds." "I'll apply for this job when I get a car." What you are saying is "I'm waiting to get my sh*t together until I get my sh*t together. (Read that again.) We are all guilty of this, so I'm not pointing fingers. However, I am telling you to snap out of it! We have to learn how to be happy with our NOW so that we will be able to take the baby steps required to reach our goals.

Can you imagine how many people suffer unhappily every day waiting on something to happen to solidify their happiness?

Did you know that the richest place in the world is the cemetery? This is a representation of three things: 1) People were unaware of their gifts and talents. 2) People were afraid to share their gifts. 3) People were waiting until "the right time" to share their gifts.

Truth is many of us won't share our gifts because we are crippled by fear and the thoughts and opinions of others. We are afraid of failing and we are afraid of people knowing that we have failed. For this reason, many of us will never birth the gift that we were created to share. But imagine the greatness that could happen if you stopped allowing fear to rule you. What would happen if you birthed and nurtured your gifts? Who's life could be changed? Who would benefit from your calling?

Let's be honest, it's tough when you are called to do something that you've never done, but it's not impossible. The key to creating a life of freedom is knowing what you want and having the confidence to go out and get it! No matter what lemons life hands you, always be willing to make lemonade! Your past has a purpose and this purpose is aligned with your destiny! If you are ready to receive everything that this life has to offer, you must be ready to take risks!

Here are three of my fave famous figures that took a risk at living their best life!

Beyonce- Via www.brit.co/

When Beyoncé dropped her surprise album at the end of 2013, she took the world by storm. Every girl's new favorite song was "Drunk in Love." Queen Bey, however, was terrified of what feedback she might receive. Dropping an entire album at once without any prior promotion is a big risk, even if you are Beyoncé. Naturally, though, her album was amazing, and Beyoncé went down as one of the most fabulous risk-takers in history.

Taraji P. Henson-Via HerAgenda Blog

It was not until moving to Los Angeles with only $700 to her name and a young son, that Henson was able to start her career as a professional actress. "People thought I was crazy." Henson told PEOPLE of deciding to leave her lucrative job back home in Washington, D.C. to take a shot at making it big in Hollywood.

After graduating from Howard University, Henson was working as a supervisor on a five-star dining cruise when she packed up her son, Marcel, and moved to California at the age of 26. "My dad knew that acting was my calling," says Henson. "One day, he looked at me and said, 'How do you expect to catch fish on dry land? You have to go where the jobs are.' So I moved out here."

After almost two years of auditioning, in 1997, at the age of 27 Henson first appeared on the small screen playing a 16 year old on the show The Parenthood. That moment followed a consistent stream of small guest and recurring roles on sitcoms like Smart Guy and Sister Sister. In 2001, she finally landed her breakout movie role opposite Tyrese Gibson in the film Baby Boy.

Tiffany Haddish- Via People.com Blog

Tiffany Sarah Haddish hails from Los Angeles, California and before her breakout role in Girls Trip, her talent can be seen on shows such as OWNs, If Loving You Is Wrong and The Carmichael Show. Haddish, the oldest of five siblings, is no stranger to tough times as a kid. At an early age, she assumed the role of caregiver to her mom and younger siblings after her mother was involved in a traumatic car accident that she later found out was caused by her Step-Father severing the break line in the vehicle. Her childhood was filled with depression, foster homes, and even a near death experience with toxic shock syndrome. Despite the hand she was dealt, like a phoenix from the ashes, she rose. Tiffany Haddish used comedy as her escape and she turned her pain into a paycheck.

In an interview with Vanity Fair, Haddish opens up about her early career days, when she lived out of her car, and how fellow comedian Kevin Hart gave her the motivation — and money —she needed to move her life and career in a new direction.

Using the money Hart gave her, Haddish booked a room at a local motel. She says Hart told her that once she got a place to stay, she should write out her goals and start doing something every day towards making them happen.
"I wrote: Get myself an apartment. Do these things, all these people I wanna work with, everything," she says. "I pretty much tackled almost all those goals."

What are three things that you could do today to push you closer to your end goal? It doesn't have to be major. It could be something as simple as waking up a little earlier each day or writing your goals out on paper. Keep it simple but specific.

"You have to fight to reach your dream. You have to sacrifice and work hard for it."

Lionel Messi

What are you willing to sacrifice for your dreams? Ex: partying on the weekends.

*"If you believe that you've got all that you need to succeed in this life, then it is true.
If you do not believe this, then that is also true.
Perception is a major key to manifesting the life you want."*

Mone' Wallace

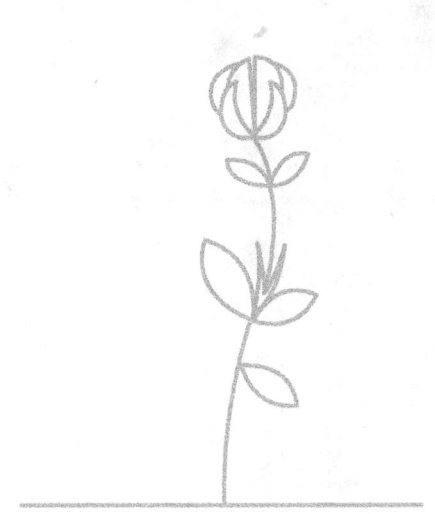

Chapter 10

What If I Told You...

The one thing that remains true is this, there's one reason why people neglect the opportunity to live the life that they truly desire. This is fear. This is what cripples us from doing so many things in life. We are fearful of failure, we are fearful of opinions, we are fearful of being told "I told you so." We fear that if we drop out of college to follow our dreams, people are going to look at us as if we're crazy. We fear that if we don't live the life that Mom and Dad plan for us they're going to be mad at us forever. We fear that leaving a relationship to find out who we truly are is selfish. We eat, sleep and breathe fear...and that is what keeps so many of us living an unhappy life. Because when you live in a state of fear, you stay in a safety net. Your life becomes repetitive and you just repeat the same things over and over, because you are too fearful to step outside of everything that you've ever known.

What if I told you that you already have all that you need to succeed in this life? You have your gifts, talents and resources to help you create your ideal life. Manifesting this ideal life consists of belief, effort and consistency. When you combine these three keys with your skills and talent, you become unstoppable!

Nothing that you do is for nothing. Every experience, job, relationship, friendship and interaction has left you with something. Whether it be a skill or a story that taught you a lesson. Even a broken heart or an unforgettable smile, they are all experiences that something can be learned from. My belief is that everything we experience in this life is for gain. From day to day we have to be conscious of our interactions. Start paying attention to your conversations, are they positive or negative? What new skill did you learn today at the job you can't stand? Who made you smile simply because they smiled at you? There is always something to be learned. Even the simplest moments can teach us the greatest lessons if we are aware and open to receive it as such.

Everything that we've experienced in life has prepared us for a greater purpose and it is up to us to answer our calling and serve. Whether it be to help others solve a problem or to simply make someone feel good, what are your gifts and talents? On this next page, I want you to take some time to think about your talents, gifts, and skills. Then on the next sheet of paper I want you to write down your passions. I want you to write on one side your good passions. For example, "I absolutely love doing hair, I couldn't see myself doing anything else, I'd even do it for free if I had to." And on the other side, I want you to write your negative passions. For example, "It really burdens my heart to see how our young black kings are being treated in America today and I am ready to be a part of the resolution." Combining your passion, your skills, your talents, and your gifts is what will make room for you. I do believe that we are all here for a purpose. And that main purpose is to serve someone other than ourselves. So whatever your gifts may be, whatever your talents may be, stop waiting for validation and approval. God has already given you all that you need to thrive in this life. It'd be a slap in the face for you to NOT live your best life.

What are your gifts and talents?

How can you use your gifts to serve others?

Who would benefit from your gifts? (Be specific)

*"You are an acquired taste.
Once you realize your worth
you'll stop giving people discounts."*

Mone' Wallace

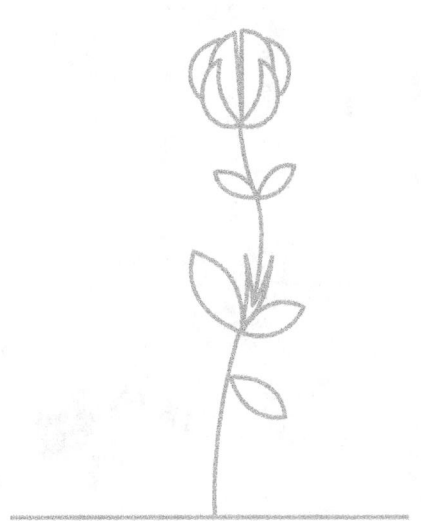

Chapter 11

Stop Giving Discounts!

From a very young age, many women are taught to be submissive. Maybe we didn't know what it was at the time, but we were slowly being trained on how to allow the world to run over us. There is a difference between speaking your truth and speaking disrespectfully. And I don't know about you, but for me, from the time that I was a young girl I was always told to stay in a child's place. Which I'm sure most of us were and I can admit I was pretty sassy, but most times I can recall just speaking my truth. But after so many times of being quieted, it became normal for me to just stay quiet. This is when I became voiceless. But as I stated, these things stay with you. As I became a teenager, I didn't speak up about things that bothered me so much. Then as I entered adulthood, I realized I didn't know how to communicate or I just wouldn't communicate. In losing your voice you lose the ability to be able to speak up for yourself. You lose the ability to say things like, "I'm worth more than that." You also lose your power when you lose your voice.

Many times, I found myself in different relationships where I allowed things to happen that I knew were not right, but I didn't have the courage to speak up. I remember being in an argument with my ex and every time I voiced how I felt he would say things like, "you're being judgmental" or, "what you're saying right now isn't really important." These type of comments can really destroy you if you accept them. Well, for me I accepted these comments often. So as an adult, it was very hard for me to communicate how I felt when I disagreed with something; because I didn't want people to think that I was trying to be difficult. I no longer believed that the things I had to say were of any importance. This is how we end up giving away discounts. When you lose your voice and the power to say things like, "I deserve better," you allow that man that you love so much to continue to put his hands on you, to cheat on you, to treat your kids as if they were animals. There are so many different examples that could be used there, but hopefully you get my drift. You are worth so much more than settling for anything less than the best. Lastly, you are one of God's greatest creations, you roam this Earth raining royalty, you are walking and breathing pure greatness and you deserve only the best life, the best love, and the best vacations with your girls.

Today is the day that you stop being quiet. Today, I want you to practice standing up for yourself. I want you to face your mirror, look yourself in the mirror and tell yourself, "I am no longer giving discounts on what I deserve. This applies in my personal and professional life, say it again! "I am no longer giving discounts on what I deserve!"

Whether it's love, business, or friendships, you've got to be totally raw and real with you. You have got to know what value you have. You have got to know who you truly are in order to be able to tell people who you are. I challenge you to dig deep inside and ask who you are at your core and what your needs are. I truly believe that what you want, you can have…whatever it is! If you have a vision for that man or woman, that house or car, that job, that career, or that dream life, go after it! Whatever Vision you have, you have the power to make it come true. You have the power to manifest all great things and abundance in your life. But it starts with your belief system. The only way that you can truly manifest things into your life is to truly believe that you deserve them and to become the person that truly does deserve them.

What makes you valuable?

What do you bring to the table in any relationship, partnership, or friendship?

What are your strengths?

_____

_____

_____

_____

_____

_____

_____

What are your weaknesses?

_____

_____

_____

_____

_____

_____

_____

Put this somewhere where you can see it every single day. This will be a constant reminder of how valuable you truly are so that you would stop giving discounts on your life.

"It does not matter how slowly you go as long as you do not stop."

Confucius

Chapter 12

YOU are ENTIRELY up to YOU

Everything that we do in this life is according to our ambition, our actions, and our drive. It's nice to be able to depend on other people sometimes, but when it comes to living your life on purpose you've got to be very intentional. I had to go through a point where I've had to take myself out of the victim role. Because what I've learned is this: when we claim the role of being a victim we are choosing to give our power away. But when we heal from situations that once held us bound and we remove ourselves from being the victim, we now have gained our power back. By taking full accountability for your life, your thoughts, and your actions, you are taking full responsibility and making a commitment to yourself to do better.

You are the only one who knows what you want. You are the only one who knows what that vision in your head looks like. You are the only one that can make anything happen for you in this lifetime. My favorite word has truly become accountability. Because if we take accountability for our lives, our thoughts and actions will be able to fix the things that we once thought were unfixable or out of our power. When I started taking accountability for why I was losing friends, why my relationships weren't working, and why I was still unhappy about things that had happened in my past, I felt powerful. I was able to forgive so many people and truly evolve into this woman that I am and still becoming, because I have learned how to take true accountability for my life. Therefore, being able to make the necessary changes.

You are totally responsible for your own happiness. I know we as women want to say this person makes me happy. And trust me there's absolutely nothing wrong with saying that. However, be sure that you were happy or are going to be happy while you're in this relationship and if this relationship should end. I remember being so in love that I thought he was my only reason for being happy. I'd fallen so deep in love with everything that he said, everything that he did, and every move that he made that nothing he could do was wrong. I made excuses for him and his behavior even when I truly didn't believe him myself. I entered that relationship with so many insecurities and so much baggage, but I expected him to fix me. I had made my life all about his life and that's when I lost myself. So for four years (five to be exact), I held onto the thoughts of "what if" and "maybe." I dated and got into other relationships, but it was only to allow time to pass. I never stopped thinking about what if.

It wasn't until I took accountability for the part that I played in our relationship that I was able to forgive him, forgive myself, and truly move on from that. Taking full accountability for my actions meant I knew that I was wrong for getting into a relationship when I had not healed from my last one. This also meant that I was wrong for depending on him to fix me when that was never his job. The mistake is we idolize people, we become lustful over people and we tend to put them on this pedestal. Then once they fall down and disappoint us, we become so hurt and broken and we feel obligated for them to make it up to us. But if we truly took accountability for our own actions and if we could truly be honest with ourselves and ask ourselves the questions that may be a little embarrassing for us to answer, but are so necessary for us to get to the bottom of Our truth, then we will be able to heal all the hurt and forgive all that we thought was unforgivable.

You are totally up to you, babe, and whatever it is that you want I promise you can have it. It is right at the tip of your fingers. You are ready to transform your life into the best one that you've ever experienced and it is right in front of you! It is attainable and it is waiting on you to become the woman that truly wants and deserves it. Everything that you've ever dreamt to have is possible and you've got all that you need inside of you to make it happen. There is nothing but you stopping you from being this woman that you wish to be, living the life that you want to live, and having the love that you wish to have.

I want you to make the best decision for your life. I want you to WIN! But what does this look like for you? Close your eyes and imagine what life would truly look like if you were to live in total freedom, living authentically in your truth. Enjoying the carefree blissful life, unbothered by the opinions and judgement of others. Are you ready to create this life? Let's dig in to some Q&A.

What would your life look like if you were to live authentically in your truth?

_____
_____
_____
_____

What do envision when you hear the word freedom?

_____
_____
_____
_____

How badly do you want this new life?

_____
_____
_____
_____

What radical thing are you willing to do in order to propel you into this life?

_____
_____
_____
_____

NOW LET'S GET TO WERK!

If you are ready to redefine your life and start living a life of authenticity and true freedom, it requires one very important thing! You being committed to you! You have all that you need to become the woman that your soul says HELL YES to every single day! Make it happen!

About the Author

Mone' Wallace was born in Staten Island, New York and has been a proud resident of Augusta, Georgia for over fifteen years. She is a thirty year young sassy diva who is witty, funny, and all out authentic. Her passion is to help women WIN in life! She is an author, speaker, and mentor who has dedicated her life to helping women evolve and rediscover their true identity. Having overcome heartbreak, abuse, molestation and failure, she'd fallen into a deep place of depression. For over five years she remained in a sunken place and just as she reached her wits end, she attempted suicide. Luckily, God had other plans for her life. After this failed attempt, she finally decided to submit fully to her higher power and in doing so, she found the healing she'd been yearning for. After spending months in isolation, getting to know herself and understand who she was called to be, she had a vision of what her life could be. At that moment, she decided that she wanted to share her story with the hope of helping other women to overcome these same obstacles. She has now turned her life from tragedy to triumph and she plans to share with other women how to heal those broken places so that they may also find their peace and power. Through her books, webinars, seminars and coaching, she plans to educate, inspire and encourage women to indulge in self-awareness, self-love and self-care so that they may be in tune with their inner spirit and truly live in joy and abundance. Her goal is to help one million women rediscover the truth of who they are, before life happened and before society told them who they are or should be. Another goal is to also help women find their voice, activate their power and position into purpose.

www.ingramcontent.com/pod-product-compliance
Lightning Source LLC
Chambersburg PA
CBHW080350170426

43194CB00014B/2745